Don't Be Afraid Of The Dark

Ericka Siyo

Presentation by *BookLeaf Publishing*

Web: www.bookleafpub.com

E-mail: info@bookleafpub.com

ISBN: 9789395890854

First edition 2022

DEDICATION

To Nicole, and Michel

ACKNOWLEDGEMENT

A big thank you to Book Leaf Publishing for this
wonderful opportunity.

I've Tried

I've tried.
I've tried
I've tried, God knows I've tried!
To do as they say.
Eat my five a day.
Go to bed early.
Run, walk, and stop watching TV.
I've tried.
God knows I've tried!
To be as good as they can be.
Stop drinking coffee.
Walk my cats and dogs
But here we go...
I love my fags and rhum coco.
My cheese, chocolate and late nights in.
Without my sins I wouldn't be.
I will die young but happy,
And no matter what they say,
It is better than getting old and grumpy.

The Muffin And The Mosquito

Like a muffin on a mosquito,
You are my Ohio because I love you so.
Like a muffin on a mosquito,
You are my winter snow because I miss you so.
Like a muffin on a mosquito, you are my deep
blue sea because I need you so.
Can't you see? You mean the world to me!
Like a muffin on a mosquito, you are the Ohio
that I promise to love, cherish and care for, until
death comes and knocks at our door.
Like a muffin on a mosquito, I'll share your
laughter and dry your tears, and if you have
enough of me, or if I break my vows, then I'll let
you go.
Like a muffin on a mosquito, my love for you is
shining like the sun heats and grows your
hundred rose gardens.
Like a muffin on a mosquito, you are my Ohio
because I love so.

The Park

I'm walking in the park,
And I think you know,
Just how I feel.
The time that past,
And the thing that were;
Should never be unreal.
How do you feel?
Tell me, how do you feel?
When days like this seem so unreal.
I'm walking in the park,
And I remember, as I walk past,
The way we were and the things we did.
Now years have gone by,
And our youth is behind.
You've gone yours ways,
And I've gone mine.
Life is a journey
Where we shouldn't look back,
Even if the destination is painful and dark.
I'm walking in the park,
And I think you know,
Just how I feel.
The time that past,
And the things that were;
Should never be unreal.

Regrets

I'm sorry, I wasn't ready.
For you, for us.
I pushed you away,
And I cry everyday.
I wish I could go back
To that first moment
Where we've met.
Where a bright spark
Shone through your eyes,
Where your smile melted my heart.
I'm sorry my love,
I wish I could call you mine.
I feel like an empty glass.
I ran like a coward,
And left you behind.
And when I returned,
I ran away again.
Leaving you in tears,
And ashamed.
I'm so sorry my love,
I had to burn,
And when the light entered,
You moved on to another.
I shall regret you forever,
I will never call you mine,
To my biggest shame.

Driving Away From Life

So we get married,
We have kids
We buy cars and houses
We run to work to pay our bills.
But who are we?
We live our lives in wealth or poverty.
We run, we run, we run
Thinking we'll always be,
Stronger to biology.
We make life hell,
Where it is just a simple matter
Of breathing air and Carpe Diem.
Life is a great place to be,
For anyone and anything.
There shouldn't be a place
For loneliness and cruelty.
We won't take our cars
To our graves.
We drive away from life
Where we should just be.
We ignore who we are,
And our friends next door.
We drive this world crazy.
But the question remain,
Why do we do this to ourselves?
The answer lays into our hearts.

Cristmases Alone

Hundreds years old
I feel the years in my bones
I spend my Christmases alone
My friends and family are gone.
I still feel joy in my heart
When I see young hearts in love
It reminds me of my past
That I look back with a smile.
Now it's me with my whisky
And my cat Snoopy.
My house is full of memory of joy
With kids running all around.
The years have gone by pretty fast,
Now my life is in the past.
I wonder when the good Lord,
Will show up at my door,
So I can hear my husband,
Calling me love.
So, I just sit there waiting,
For my time to come,
Seizing my last days
With little things and simple joy.

Disillusioned Love

Claire stared out the window,
Watching as the snowflakes lazily drifted to the
ground.
She sighed, her heart heavy with sadness.
It had been two weeks since Sebastien had told
her he didn't love her.
Two long weeks of emptiness and loneliness.
She loved Sebastien more than anything else.
And it hurt so much to be rejected by him.
She had begged him to change his mind,
But he refused to listen.
He said that he just wasn't feeling it for her.
Claire couldn't help but feel like, She was being
punished for something.
She had no idea what she could have done
wrong,
But she was determined to win back Sebastien's
love.
She was going to do whatever it took,
Whereas, she should have just, let it go...

Single Mum

My name is Janet.
I am sitting on the edge of my bed, feeling numb.
My husband has just left me for someone twenty-five years younger.
I am now on my own with three children to look after.
I feel like I have been hit by a truck.
I can't quite wrap my head around what had just happened.
I want to cry, but the tears just don't come.
Instead, I sit there in silence, trying to make sense of it all.
I'm not sure what the future hold for me and my kids, but I know one thing: I'm not going to give up on hope.
I will fight for them tooth and nail, and do whatever it takes to ensure they are happy and safe.
Even if it means being a single mom for the rest of my life, I am determined to make it work.

Bye Bye Ciggie

I love smoking.
There's nothing like the feeling of taking a drag
from a cigarette,
Letting the smoke fill my lungs.
It's relaxing, calming, and I love it.
Cigarettes are killing me though,
Every day, they're slowly chipping away at my
life,
And I can't keep doing this to myself.
I've tried quitting smoking before,
But it's been so hard.
I always end up going back to cigarette.
This time, I'm really going to try to quit
I know it won't be easy,
But I'm determined.
Every day, I tell myself that I'm not going to
smoke anymore.
And every day, I fail miserably.
But I'm not going to give up.
I know that someday, I'll finally be able to quit
smoking for good!
Ciggie, you won't get me!!

Freedom And Innocence

He was finally free.
Twenty years of his life had been taken away
from him,
But it was all over now.
He could feel the sun on his face,
The wind in his hair,
And he was happy.
There was a fear inside him,
A fear of what awaited him,
In this wild and cruel world.
He was old now,
On his own.
He didn't know where to go,
Or what to do.
But he would find a way.
He always had.
After all,
Freedom is the ability
To think your own life.

Aloneness

At first it was hard,
To be alone.
No-one to talk to,
No friends to go out with.
My poor health,
Made me live like an hermit.
I had to survive on my own.
I turned my back on those,
Who weren't good for me.
I was left with only myself,
For company.
So I found refuge in my dreams,
And I started to write poetry.
Until I realised, it carried me.
I have found myself
In loneliness,
And now I can say clearly,
I know what is like to be alone,
But most of all,
I am happy!

The Gifted Child

I was always the kid at school who couldn't stay still.
My teachers would get mad at me because I never listened,
And I was always daydreaming.
They said I had some kind of mental health disorder,
Yes, I was different.
I loved music.
I loved jumping up and down to the rhythm of soul and blues.
Today, I am a choreographer.
And when I tell my story, people often look at me with judgment,
But I'm proud of myself.
It's not easy to follow your passions, even if they're unconventional.

I Miss You So Much

Gil sat on the floor of her room, surrounded by
pictures of her and her dad.
They were taken everywhere:
At the zoo, at the park, at the beach. She missed
him so much.
It felt like a part of her was missing,
Now that he was gone.
She thought back to the last time she saw him.
He had been so sick and weak.
But he had still tried to smile for her. "I'm sorry,
Daddy," she whispered through her tears. "I'm
trying my best."
She wished she could go back in time and
change things.
If only she had known how sick he was...maybe
she could have said goodbye properly.
But it was too late now.
He was gone forever,
And she would never see him again.

The Journey

"Life is a journey, my son,"
John explained to his young boy.
"There are going to be good times and bad
times, but it's all worth it in the end."
The boy looked up at his father with wide eyes,
taking in his words.
"Really?" he asked.
 John nodded solemnly.
"Yes, really. It's not always easy, but it's worth
it."
He put an arm around his son and gave him a
hug.
"Just keep that in mind, okay?"
The boy smiled and nodded before burying his
head in his father's chest.
John could feel the warmth of his son's love
spreading through him,
Filling him with happiness.
Yes, life was definitely a journey – and he was
grateful for every step of the way.

Locked Up Outside

Twenty-one today,
No birthday cake,
I'm lucky if I can get,
A chicken nuggets,
My mum abandoned me,
My dad doesn't care,
My friend run away,
No need to mention no family.
Nowhere to go,
No-one to turn to,
What did I do to deserve this?
I don't know.
I flew domestic violence,
Only to find street violence.
I'm locked up outside,
And I'm scared.
I dream of charming prince,
But he only exists,
In fairy tales.
What can I do to turn my life around?
If only someone gave me a chance!
But from where I'm coming from,
No-one opens their doors.
Locked up outside,
It's my destiny,

I'll end up beaten up by some junkies.
Twenty-one today,
My life is over!

Seize The Day

"No matter what you're going through, seize the day."

Stacy looked her friend in the eyes with a seriousness that couldn't be denied. "Don't let your problems consume you. Take some time for yourself, and enjoy life."

Her friend gave her a weak smile in return, before turning away and resuming their walk.

Stacy hoped that her words would sink in, that her friend would take her advice to heart.

It was so easy to get lost in your own head, especially when things were tough.

But it was important to remember that there was more to life than just your problems.

Stacy knew this from experience.

She had been through her share of trials and tribulations, but she had never stopped fighting. And she never would – not as long as she still had breath in her body.

So she urged her friend on, telling herself that everything would be okay. Because it always was – eventually

Twenty-one Today

"Thanks for the offer, man,"
I said with a smile.
I was clutching the greasy bag of chicken
nuggets tightly.
It was my only birthday present this year.
"I really appreciate it."
The owner of the takeaway restaurant smiled
back at me.
 "Don't mention it. I remember what it's like to
be starting out at your age. Here, take this job as
my gift to you."
My face lit up with happiness.
I couldn't believe my luck!
This was the best birthday present I'd ever
received.
 "Thank you so much!"
I exclaimed, wrapping my arms around the
owner's waist in a hug.
Years sleeping rough,
And my nightmare was finally over!

A Better Place

We seek a better place,
We think it's out there,
But our better place;
Is already there.
It's hidden in our eyes,
Who can't see through the dark.
Only, if we looked closely,
We'll see, the beauty of a rose,
The magic of the sun,
Who heals our bleeding wounds.
We'll hear the whisper of the trees,
Telling us to breath slowly, calmly,
Until we find peace of mind.
Only if we stopped for a minute,
Screaming and shouting at each other,
We'll realise, we're all brothers.
Don't you think it's time,
To let our grudges behind?
The world is a pretty place to be,
And the sun shines for everybody.
It's only a shame,
That we cannot see,
For what it is truly,
And that we keep blaming each other,
For what we have made of it.